Great Drives

22 Great Irish Roads

Great Drives

22 Great Irish Roads

Bob Montgomery

Dreoilín

Other books by the same author:
An Irish Roadside Camera 1896-1906 – The Pioneering years
The 1903 Irish Gordon Bennett – the Race that saved Motorsport
Down Many a Road – The Story of Shell in Ireland
An Irish Roadside Camera 1907-1918 – The Years of Growth
Racing in the Park – 100 Years of Motor Racing in Dublin's Phoenix Park
A Lifetime's Collecting - The Legendary Car Collection of Jim Boland

Dreoilín Transport Album Series:
Early Motoring in Ireland
Leslie Porter – Ireland's Pioneer Racing Driver
The Irish International Grand Prix 1929-31
The Phoenix Park Speed Trials 1903
The Irish Gordon Bennett Race 1903
Ford manufacture and Assembly at Cork 1919-1984
R J Mecredy – The Father of Irish Motoring

Published by Dreoilín Specialist Publications Limited,
Tankardstown, Garristown, County Meath, Ireland.
Telephone: (00353) 1 8354481
e-Mail: info@dreoilin.ie

Trade enquiries to Gill & MacMillan,
Telephone (00353) 1 5009500

First published in April 2011

Text and photographs copyright © 2011 Bob Montgomery (except where stated).
ISBN 978-1-902773-24-7
A CIP record is available for this title from the British Library.

All rights reserved. No part of this publication may be reproduced or transmitted in any form including photocopy, recording, or any information storage and retrieval system, without prior permission from the publishers in writing.

Design by Alan Pepper Design.
Set in Weiss by Alan Pepper Design and printed in the Republic of Ireland by Walsh Colour Print.

See our full range of books at
www.dreoilin.ie

Introduction

When a short series of articles about interesting roads in Ireland was first contemplated in *The Irish Times*, my first reaction was that this was the perfect opportunity to demonstrate that motoring on this over-regulated isle of ours could still be memorable, and most of all could still be fun.

That this could be so was soon apparent from the reactions of readers who responded with letters and e-mails about my choices of roads and often suggesting their own favourites. This strong interaction with readers became a feature of the series for me, and it was the many, many suggestions from them about "when will there be a book of the series" that has led to this publication. For this first volume of 'Great Drives', I've gathered together 22 articles representing all of the six series to date. A major advantage of presenting them in this format is that the photographs can now be reproduced in their full glory, often together with extra photographs that space did not allow in their original publication in *The Irish Times*.

The other thing that became a feature of the series was the cars that I drove. I really don't know if this was because I tended to use unusual cars or if it was because they tended to be of a sporting nature, but once again there was a strong reader reaction, all of which was very positive. For this reason I've included at the end of this book a few notes on the cars used in the chosen articles.

I'd like to thank Michael McAleer, Editor of the MOTORS section in *The Irish Times* for his original suggestion for the series back in 2005, and for permission to reproduce the articles and the accompanying maps created by *The Irish Times* Map Department.

Finally, I do hope you enjoy this compilation, and more importantly, driving the roads they detail. As always, I will be delighted to receive your comments and suggestions.

Bob Montgomery,
April 2011.

1. Glendine Gap

A PLACE OF STUNNING BEAUTY

One of the great pleasures of writing this column is the discovery of hitherto unknown (to the author at least) roads.

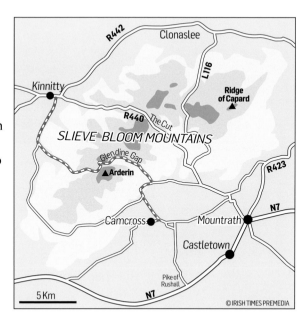

I've previously written of the road from Clonaslee to Mountrath, which travels across the Slieve Bloom Mountains *via* The Cut, and for this column I returned to the same region. The Slieve Bloom Mountains are something of a peculiarity, rising up from the flat midlands of Ireland to quite respectable heights.

As so often happens in Ireland, one can turn off the old main Dublin – Limerick road, travel just a few short kilometers and be in a totally different environment, almost devoid of traffic and human habitation.

I started my journey at the Pike of Rushall, that evocatively-named crossroads on the N7 just a short distance to the west of Castletown. Initially, I followed the brown signposts for the Poet's

Deep in the beautiful wooded Glendine Gap.

7

This wonderful road is unique in an Irish landscape context.

> *'This is a wonderful road through a landscape more reminiscent of Bavaria that of Ireland's midlands.'*

Cottage in the mountain village of Camross. However, instead of turning left at Camross cross-roads, I continued straight ahead for almost two kilometers until I came to a left turn marked by an unmistakable sign reading 'Road hazardous in winter'.

This is the start of a truly spectacular road that climbs over the Glendine Gap and on towards the village of Kinnitty.

From its start, the road quickly begins to climb through a densely wooded valley, a feature that may often serve to obscure the beauty of the place. However, here – and indeed along most of this road – it serves only to enhance the stunning beauty of the valley and the many panoramic views that can be glimpsed through the trees.

Onward and upward, the road rises through the valley. It was noticeable when we traversed the road that it was sprinkled throughout by small stones, washed down from the surrounding hillsides by recent heavy rains. Such small irritations aside, this is a wonderful road through a landscape more reminiscent of Bavaria that of Ireland's midlands.

The Killeen River runs close to the road during most of the ascent towards Glendine Gap, while Arderin rises to 527m to the southwest of the road. To the north, both Carroll's Hill (428m) and Stillbrook Hill (496m) tower over the road.

The boundary between Counties Laois and Offaly is marked by this stone near the top of the Glendine Gap.

The densely wooded valley only enhances the stunning beauty of the valley and the many panoramic views that can be glimpsed through the trees.

All too soon, the road's highpoint is reached, marked by a monument that also marks the border between Laois and Offaly. Climbing to Glendine Gap, the views are increasingly spectacular, while once over the highest point of the road, the landscape is gentler as the road descends towards its meeting with the road into Kinnitty.

The road on the Offaly side of Glendine Gap is not as good as that on the southern - or Laois - side of the drive, and care should be taken in places where there are some large pot holes. During the two hours or so that I spent in an unhurried exploration along this road, I met no cars whatsoever, which is remarkable, considering that at no time was I ever more than ten or fifteen minutes' drive from the busy N7.

Glendine Gap was certainly an unexpected discovery for me, and I would go so far as to unhesitatingly place it among the top ten roads I've written about in this series. Without travelling far, its possible to get away from all signs of civilization along this fine road and to enjoy a landscape quite different to others on this island.

2. *Slieve Croob*

QUIET COUNTRY LANES GENTLY FOLDED INTO THE LANDSCAPE

If you like meandering down quiet country lanes gently folded into the landscape, then the part of Ireland we're exploring this week is probably just right for you. Glimpsed in the distance while near Castlewellan for a previous article in this series, Slieve Croob (534m) rises due south of Belfast in the rolling County Down countryside.

Around 420 million years ago the rocks that form this landscape were created and large volumes of molten rock, or magma, were generated at depth. Here, unlike in parts of, for example, Tyrone, much of it remained underground and cooled slowly into the hard igneous rock called granodiorite, that today forms much of Slieve Croob.

The Legananny Dolmen, said to be the most photographed in Ireland.

11

Through the 'window' of this interesting monument can be viewed the source of the River Lagan.

'*What is fascinating about the view from Windy Gap is the way in which it forms a watershed between several quite different types of landscape.*'

I approached the area around Slieve Croob from the B175 road that runs from Castlewellan to Ballynahinch, turning off at the sign for Drumkeeragh Forest. This is soon reached and by then the eastern slopes of Slieve Croob were rising to the west of our road. By continuing along this road and bearing left at the next crossroads, we arrived at a junction just outside the tiny village of Finnis. Again veering left we continued on this road until we reached the car park provided at the gap between Slieve Croob and the smaller Cratlieve or Legananny Mountain (429m). From this car park one can walk the short distance to the top of Slieve Croob where there are several masts.

In the car park is an interesting monument through part of which one can view the source of the River Lagan. In addition, there are fine views in a northerly direction over the rolling County Down countryside towards the city of Belfast.

By continuing on this road to the next junction and bearing right again at the following junction one comes to the Legananny Dolmen, named after *Liagán Áine* and meaning the 'pillar stone of Anya', the mythological mother goddess loved by the warrior Finn McCool.

Dating from 2500-2000 BC, the capstone of the Legananny Dolmen balances elegantly on three

12

To the south of our road the Mourne Mountains rise in dramatically rugged fashion.

unusually tall and thin upright stones and is a favourite with tourists and photographers visiting the area. We continued along this road until we turned right at the next junction followed by two left turns at subsequent junctions. This brought us to the Windy Gap on the slopes of Slievenaboley Mountain (324m). There is here another car park and picnic area and towards the south are magnificent views towards the Mourne Mountains. What is fascinating about the view from Windy Gap is the way in which it forms a watershed between several quite different types of landscape.

To the south the Mourne Mountains rise in dramatically rugged fashion. To the east is Slieve Croob where the River Lagan rises before its short run to the sea at Belfast, while over the high ground of Slievenaboley Mountain and Deehommed Mountain to the northwest the mountain-scape gives way to a patchwork of small green fields stretching as far as the eye can see.

In this short exploration we've just touched upon a few of the main attractions of this area, but there is far more to see and explore. It's a gently – for the most part – rolling landscape that meanders around Slieve Croob. The surrounding hills will form the basis of a very pleasant day spent exploring should you drive this way.

3. Gap of Dunloe

A PLACE OF WILD BEAUTY

Many years ago I traversed the Gap of Dunloe while servicing during a Circuit of Ireland Rally. The experience has stayed with me down the years for two reasons: the sheer difficulty of the drive over what were then unsurfaced roads and the otherworldly nature of the place itself.

Knowing that a surfaced road had now replaced the road over which I travelled I've been keen to once again cross this most famous of Kerry passes. Thus it was that I found myself turning off the N72 just west of Fossa at the signpost for Beaufort and the Gap of Dunloe.

After several kilometers, having passed the Dunloe Ogham stones, which were once the roof of a souterrain – an underground passage – that collapsed at the end of the 19th century, a few kilometers further on is the hive of tourist activity that surrounds Kate

One of the most dramatic sights in Ireland – the road rising up to the famous Gap of Dunloe.

15

Everywhere are giant boulders that have fallen from the slopes of Purple Mountain to the east of the road.

'*Sadly, a thick mist descended before I had an opportunity to spot any of these majestic birds, whose presence, one instinctively feels, so appropriate to this landscape.*'

Kearney's Cottage, and from where the jarvey-men take customers over the Gap on their jaunting cars.

It is shortly after this spot that the Gap of Dunloe begins to reveal itself in its wild beauty. Beside the road are a series of small, black lakes – the first being appropriately if unimaginatively called 'Black Lake' followed by 'Cushnavally' and finally 'Auger Lake'. Joined by the River Loe, the road continues to climb along the edges of these lakes and a very spectacular view of the actual mountain pass beckons one further up the valley. Everywhere are giant boulders that have fallen from the slopes of Purple Mountain (793m) to the east or from the Macgillycuddy Reeks to the west.

In several places the road winds between some of these giant rocks, their sheer size reminding one of the elemental forces of nature that created this extraordinarily place. As it climbs, the road also becomes more torturous and although there are ample places to allow one to pull over to let oncoming vehicles pass, I was still surprised by the volume of traffic using this, supposedly, remote road. The road twists and turns as it reaches the Head of the Gap, from where there are fine views back towards Beaufort and across the fertile land northwest of Killarney.

Having crossed the Head of the Gap the road descends quite sharply until one meets a junction where we turned southwest to explore Black Valley. This road down into the valley comes to a

Looking towards The Black Valley.

Looking back from the road towards one of the several small, black lakes passed on the ascent.

dead end at the head of Black Valley where the heights of Broaghnabinnia rise, but my reason for taking it was the hope of seeing one of the Kerry eagles which were introduced in recent years into the area and which, I had been told, frequent the Black Valley. Sadly, a thick mist descended before I had any opportunity to spot any of these majestic birds, whose presence, one instinctively feels, so appropriate to this landscape.

Retracing my tracks back up from the Black Valley to the junction at the end of the descent from the Head of the Gap, I continued southeast towards the R568 and it's junction with Moll's Gap, from whence the N71 took me back down to Killarney.

As I've said so many times in the course of these articles, the contrast between busy roads and the wild, virtually unpopulated places I've found close by them in Ireland is quite extraordinary. It would be hard to find a greater contrast than that between the bustling town of Killarney and the wild and rugged Gap of Dunloe just a few kilometers distant. The Gap of Dunloe fully lived up to, and indeed exceeded my half-remembered memory of it from that day many years ago.

4. Mecredy's Road

GREAT ROADS, A GREAT CAR AND GOOD COMPANY – WHAT MORE COULD AN ENTHUSIASTIC DRIVER WANT?

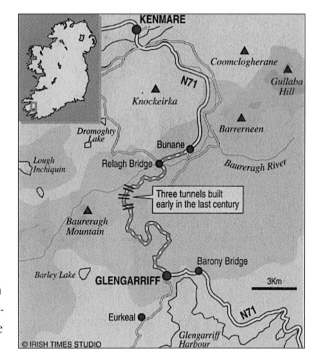

That was how I introduced this series last year. But setting out to prove that there are still roads in Ireland that could produce a great drive and bring a smile to your face, could, I imagined, turn out to be difficult. However, I need not have worried as once the search was begun more and more possibilities appeared.

Emerging from the longest of the tunnels on the N71 Kenmare to Glengarriff.

Not every road met the criteria that I laid down for inclusion. Namely, that a road chosen must be enjoyable to drive; it should have a reasonable surface; it should pass through spectacular

19

A competitor (GA Phillips in a 12 hp Humber) in the Irish Automobile Club's 1909 Reliability Trial emerges from one of the several tunnels on the N71.

'*These tunnels blasted out of the rock were considerable engineering achievements for the time.*'

scenery and have an interesting historical aspect, preferably, but not necessarily to do with motoring history.

The N71: Kenmare to Glengarriff

The road from Kenmare to Glengarriff is a road with a history. I've called it 'Mecredy's Road' for it was the genial editor of *The Motor News* who campaigned for it to be built in the first years of the last century. Mecredy saw the potential for opening up tourism in Cork and Kerry by the construction of this road and successfully used all his considerable influence as the 'Father of Motoring' in Ireland to have it built.

In truth, there had been a track there for many years but Mecredy lobbied for it to be upgraded into a proper road with graded surfaces (It was one of the first in the country to have a good surface) and featured a number of tunnels blasted out of the rock and which were considerable engineering achievements for the time. Those tunnels - virtually unchanged - are still features of Mecredy's road, the N71, today.

The Kenmare to Glengarriff road cuts across the Beara Peninsula rising slowly at first as it leaves the old town of Kenmare (Ceann Mara - The head of the Sea) which was founded in 1670 by Sir William Petty, Cromwell's surveyor-general and an ancestor of the first Marquess of Landsdowne who in 1775 planned the development of the town as a giant 'X' with two wide intersecting main streets.

On the right as the road slowly climbs is Knockkeirka (426m) while on the left are several higher peaks, among them Coomclogherane (458m), Gullaba Hill (625m) and Barrerneen (458m). Once the N71 crosses the Baurearagh River at Releagh Bridge the road becomes more interesting as it climbs and twists its way up a ridge of Baurearagh Mountain, part of the Caha Mountains that fill the centre of the Beara peninsula.

Here too, are the first of the three tunnels to be negotiated. Two are quite short, but one, at around 100 metres long, is unexpectedly long and dark. These tunnels are quite unfinished inside; the bare rock was chipped away last century, remaining now as testimony to how difficult building this road must have been. The view from the stretch of this road surrounding the tunnels is magnificent and impresses with its sheer ruggedness.

Once through the last of the tunnels the road drops down again quite quickly on the approach to Glengarriff. The Irish name for Glengarriff means 'Rugged Glen' but the modern town and its surrounds are anything but rugged. Lush woodlands and subtropical flowers warmed by the Gulf Stream make Glengarriff something special amongst Irish towns. Nowhere is this more evident than on Garinish Island, turned into an exotic garden in the 1920s by the landscape gardener, Harold Peto.

George Bernard Shaw is said to have written his play St Joan here and Garinish was gifted to the Irish People in 1953. A place of history at the end of a road of history.

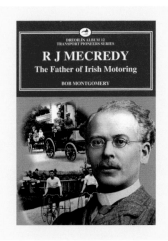

R J MECREDY

To several generations he was simply 'Arjay', and few men were as influential in the development of the cycle movement, and from 1900 onwards, in the development of motoring. Through his enthusiastic writings about the joys of touring in Ireland, first on cycles and then on cars, he probably did more in those early years than any other to develop Ireland as a tourist destination. He was involved in the 1901 Irish Motor Tour, the foundation of the Irish Automobile Club, (today the Royal Irish Automobile Club), and with bringing the AA to Ireland as well as playing a part in the early success of John Boyd Dunlop's pneumatic tyre. 'Arjay' died in 1924.

5. Ballyboughal to Drogheda (R108)

AN ANCIENT HIGHWAY TO DELIGHT AND SURPRISE

Some roads are meant to be driven, shall we say, briskly; others are born to meander along. The subject of this exploration, the R108 from Ballyboughal in North Dublin to Drogheda is a road that repays a slow meandering drive along it's length with glimpses of an ancient landscape, as the road climbs over successive hills and dales and houses betray their olden origins by lying nestled in sheltered hollows. Yet this road, today lying between other newer and busier roads, was once the route of the highway from Dublin to Newry and then on to Belfast, having been arrived at *via* Glasnevin, Santry and Forrest, just west of present-day Swords.

Taylor and Skinner's Map of 1778 contained in their seminal work *'Maps of the Roads of Ireland'* shows a road that has hardly changed today, two and a quarter centuries later. It's a landscape that shows remarkably few signs of change, the most notable being the swathe cut by the new M1 motorway which intersects the R108 a couple of kilometres north-east of Bellewstown.

An ancient landscape of meandering roads with views that surprise and delight in places north of the village of Naul.

Taylor and Skinner's map of 1778 shows a road which today has changed surprisingly little.

23

Journey's end is the impressive fortified tower at Millmount in Drogheda, site of a 12th century Norman motte.

Leaving the village of Ballyboughal one soon arrives at the foot of a gently climbing hill, where in 1925 and 1926, the Drogheda Motor Cycle Club organised a popular motorcycle hillclimb. The event must have been more of a speed trial than a hillclinb as the road chosen ran from the bridge below the present-day Hollywood Golf Club to the crossroads at Nag's Head, a distance of seven-eights of a mile with a gradient of 1 in 35. Interestingly, the reports of the event describe the finish as being at 'Knagg's Head' crossroads, the spelling being quite different to today's 'Nag's Head' – surely a case of common usage taking over from the original, Knagg having been, I believe, the name of a local family.

'The R108 now enters it's most attractive section, meandering across several hills which offer a surprisingly high view towards the sea at Balbriggan.'

Having passed Nag's Head and the ridge which is Cabinhill the road falls quite steeply into the village of Naul with it's Seamus Ennis Cultural Centre, whose restaurant is a good place to enjoy a hearty Irish breakfast! Out of Naul, the stone-age passage tomb at Fourknocks is but a short diversion to the west of the R108. It's inner chamber is some 21ft. across, far larger than Newgrange, and is well worth a look. The R108 now enters it's most attractive section, meandering across several hills which offer a surprisingly high view towards the sea at Balbriggan. In fact, the highest point on the road is but 159 metres high and later Mullaghteelin is some 148 metres above sea level. Neither hill

The Drogheda Motor Cycle Club ran a hillclimb at Knagg's Head in 1925 and 1926. This is one of the competitors in the Sidecar class.

is earth-shatteringly high but in what is generally a flat landscape they serve to give surprising elevation and a quite unexpected view to any motorist used to travelling north along the M1 or it's predecessor, the N1/R132.

Here the R108 also passes the road to Bellewstown, the site of another hillclimb course in the 1950s and today noteworthy for it's annual horse races. Soon afterwards the road drops down to intersect the M1 motorway before crossing the River Nanny and sweeping into Drogheda. Just as the road reaches Drogheda, it turns sharp right past the old Church of Ireland. However, we finish our journey on the R108 by continuing straight on at this sharp turn, coming to Millmount, an 18th century fortified tower, although the mound on which it stands is probably of Celtic origin, and was later built up by the Normans into a huge motte. In line with the road beside Millmount can be seen pedestrian steps leading down to the bridge over the River Boyne into the heart of Drogheda. Reference to Taylor and Skinner's 18th century map shows that this was the original course of the road, leading to what was then the only bridge across the river. Indeed, this remained the road until, I believe, the 1920s, and was a notorious accident black-spot.

From Ballyboughal to Millmount is just 18.8 kms, a distance that takes the modern motorist on a short journey back in time over one of the most original ancient highways remaining in this part of Ireland.

6. The Gordon Bennett Trail

IN THE TRACKS OF GIANTS

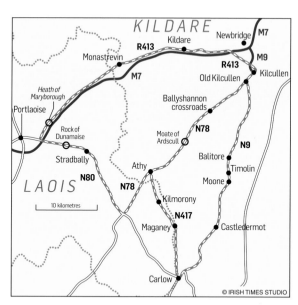

Fernand Gabriel, the Breton driver, driving his Mors during the 1903 race.

A couple of years ago the county councils of Carlow, Kildare and Laois joined together to make the route of the circuit used in the 1903 Gordon Bennett Race easily identifiable by tourists. With the passage of the 105 years since the race some of the roads have disappeared or been altered by the requirements of modern transport but more than enough of the original route and its features is still recognisable and makes the journey around the old circuit well worth while.

The route is well signposted and is divided into five stages beginning at the original start point – Ballyshannon crossroads southwest of Old Kilcullen at the end of the M9 motorway from Dublin. From the start the route first heads north-east to Old Kilcullen before swinging south on the N9 and passing through Balitore where the American team based themselves for the race, on through Timolin and Moone and through Castledermot into Carlow.

Stage two runs north-west from Carlow to Athy on the R417 passing through Maganey and Kilmorony. Athy was very much the centre of activity during the Gordon Bennett race and the Mercedes team based themselves in the town while the English team were based at Rebhan Castle

The wooded Moate of Arscull – a 13th century Norman earthworks – with the Gordon Bennett race monument in the foreground.

'*Here also, a local pioneer, Aldritt by name, attempted to fly in a plane of his own design and construction in the early years of the 20th century.*'

just a short distance away. From Athy the signs direct you back along the N78 past the start area at Ballyshannon crossroads and on to Kilcullen before turning west on the R413 to cross the Curragh Plains into Kildare town. Along the N78 you will pass the Moate of Ardscull, site of 13th century Norman earthworks – incidentally, one of the biggest of its kind in Ireland - and a particularly favoured viewing point during the race in 1903. Here, several grandstands were erected which gave a fine view of the approaching cars as they ran along one of the fastest sections of the course from Athy. Here also is the monument to the race erected in the 1960s and today a very evocative spot to sit and imagine the race cars of 1903 thundering past.

From Kildare, the Gordon Bennett route signs bring you over stage four to Monastrevin and on south-west towards Portlaoise. Monastrevin features strongly in photographs of the race and was another much-favoured spot to see the cars and their drivers close-up. After leaving Monastrevin the cars and their drivers headed out over the Heath of Maryborough, itself an important archaeological site with Iron Age burial mounds as well as Neolithic, Christian and Mediaeval sites. Here also, a local motor engineer, Aldritt by name, attempted to fly in a plane of his own design and construction in the early years of the 20th century.

The final part of the signposted route runs from the Heath to Athy swinging south-east across County Laois, passing close by The Rock of Dunamaise, an enigmatic ruin and one of the great fortresses of Ireland's past. Pause and take the time to climb its heights as the views are breathtaking on a clear day. The route passes through Stradbally and two miles outside the town occurred the one serious incident of the 1903 race when the English driver, Charles Jarrott, a great favourite of the crowd, had the steering break on his Napier while speeding on a fast downhill section. The Napier rolled and the crowd, believing both Jarrott and his riding mechanic, Bianchi, to be dead, laid them out in a nearby farmyard and covered the 'bodies' with white sheets. Imagine their surprise when the 'bodies' started to moan and speak to each other!

A couple of kilometers after Stradbally the signposts direct us north-east again through Athy and back to the finish of the route at Ballyshannon crossroads. Its a fascinating drive filled with memories of the great 1903 race which did so much to establish international motorsport once and for all.

THE 1903 IRISH GORDON BENNETT RACE
The 1903 Gordon Bennett Race came to Ireland as a result of the 1902 victory of S F Edge. The circuit chosen was a figure '8' through counties Carlow, Kildare and Laois and three circuits of one loop of the '8' and four of the other loop were run to give a total race distance of 545.8 kms. The winner was the great Belgian driver, Camille Jenatzy, driving a Mercedes car at an average speed of 49.2 mph.

Participants in a Vintage Car event gather around the Gordon Bennett memorial at Ardschull.

29

7. *Kilgarvan to Coomhola Bridge (The Shehy Mountains)*

A RUGGED DRIVE IN BARREN HILLS

In my travels around Ireland seeking out roads for this series, I have long felt that the Shehy Mountains and their surroundings in West Cork and partly in Kerry offered several interesting possibilities. Previous attempts to survey the area were ruined by torrential and persistent rain and it seemed at first as if I was to be thwarted once again on this occasion for my first attempt found me near the top of Knocknamanagh in zero visibility with no possibility of taking suitable photographs.

However an early start from Cork on the next morning proved more promising although as I traveled the N22 through Macroom and Ballyvourney the sky once again took on an increasingly ominous aspect. At Poulgorm Bridge I turned south-east along the R569 to Kilgarvan. At Kilgarvan a left turn followed very soon afterwards by a right and then a left turn had me on my intended route. At first the road appears anything but promising passing through an area of scrubland, but then we came upon our first surprise, for tucked away on this narrow road is a Motor Museum!

This is a rugged landscape with the road clinging to the mountainside for much of our journey through the Shehy Mountains.

31

The mountain sides abound in spectacular waterfalls.

'This is one of the lesser known drives in this most tourist-orientated part of our country'

This is the Kilgarvan Motor Museum of John and Joan Mitchell and their sons, a personal collection assembled over many years and on display since 1985. All of the cars are running and a visit is well worthwhile.

Resuming our journey the road now begins to rise quite quickly and the bulk of Gullaba Hill rises directly ahead. On our left is the valley of the Slaheny River across which Carran and Knockantooreen rise to 567m and 450m respectively. Our road now clings to the edge of the slopes of first Bird Hill (412m) and then Knocknamanagh ((637m) while Knockboy (680m) rises behind. A short tunnel leads us into the twistest part of the road and reveals more and more spectacular views across the valley and into the southern distance.

Eventually, the road swings to the east and climbs across a barren mountain landscape and swings around the horseshoe-shaped edges of the head of the Borlin Valley before slowly starting to

Always a rare sight – a DKW at the Kilgarvan Motor Museum.

The Kilgarvan Motor Museum was an unexpected diversion on our journey.

descend along the edges of Conigar (564m) and the other mountains at the heart of the Shehy Mountain range. The Coomhola River runs through the valley below and accompanies us for much of the long descent to our journey's end at Coomhola Bridge.

This road promised much when viewed on the map and didn't disappoint providing an interesting road through some spectacular mountain country. During my journey we met just one car supporting the thought that this is one of the lesser known drives in this most tourist-orientated part of our country. Seek it out and prepare to be surprised. Best of all, its end at Coomhola Bridge leaves us less than a kilometre away from the start of another spectacular, yet quite different drive, over 'Priest's Leap' which we'll tackle on another occasion.

8. Castlewellan's surroundings

CASTLEWELLAN'S LEAFY ROADS...

This exploration of an Irish road is not so much about a particular road as about an area. I've often travelled the road from Newry to Strangford to catch the ferry across the turbulent mouth of Strangford Lough to Portaferry, promising myself to find the time to stop and explore the area signaled by the 'brown' signs that occur half way down Castlewellan's great hill. So, on this occasion, I headed to Castlewellan to fulfill a promise to myself and to see what I could find.

What I found was an area of outstanding beauty which the road from Newry to Strangford gave little hint of, and which rewarded me with new and varied landscapes of rolling Ulster hills, green fields and leafy roads.

Our starting point was Castlewellan, a picturesque town on the northern foothills of the Mourne Mountains and through which runs the A25. Castlewellan – *Caisleán Uidhilin* or Uidhilín's Castle – is unique within Ireland for it's two main squares, each lined by chestnut trees. The unusually wide main street and it's two squares were designed by a French archi-

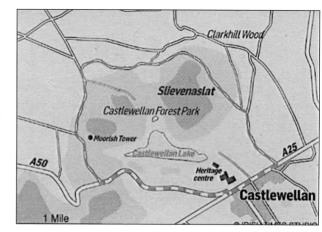

Roads over rolling Ulster hills...

Roads over the hills surrounding Castlewellan.

‘*There's an abundance of roads just waiting to be explored here so do take the time to meander and criss-cross this delightful landscape.*’

tect for the Annesley family who were the original owners of what is now Castlewellan Forest Park. Half way down the town's main street is the entrance to Castlewellan Forest Park which covers some 1100 acres and to which an entry fee is charged. The Park contains a Heritage Centre, Castle, Moorish Tower and a Maze surrounding the mile long Castlewellan Lake and is well worth taking the time to explore. The castle, built of Ballymagreehan granite in 1856 in the Scottish baronial style, overlooks the lake and was the home of the Annesley family. The forest park is also the site of Northern Ireland's National Arboretum, the core of which is a fifteen acre walled garden containing exotic and indigenous plants. Further along the A25 as one leaves Castlewellan down it's great hill is a turn to the northwest. Taking this road leads one into some of the most widely varied and beautiful countryside all packed into a relatively small area. Once again, as so often in our explorations of this island, the greatly contrasting landscapes all within a short distance of each other, are startling.

Travel anti-clockwise around the outer perimeter of Castlewellan Forest Park and its Slievenaslat (272m) and you'll encounter dramatic views as well as leafy roads that twist and turn as they rise and fall over the rolling Ulster landscape.

Leafy roads around Castlewellan.

The roads are excellent and the whole area a delight. To the north lie the mountains of Slieve Garran (391m), Cratlieve or Leganny Mountain (429m) and Slieve Croob (534m) – the source of the River Lagan, all of which we plan to return to and explore in detail on another occasion (see pages 10-13).

There's an abundance of roads just waiting to be explored here so do take the time to meander and criss-cross this delightful landscape. Around every corner, or so it seems, there's a surprise awaiting making this area, almost unknown, I suspect to southern drivers, well worth taking the time to explore and enjoy.

The landscape shows many signs of ancient habitation and there are numerous cairns, forts, raths, cashels and souterrains dotted all over the area while at Clarkill Woods is an interesting standing stone.

9. Poulaphouca Reservoir Drive

STEAM TRAMS AND SUBMERGED VILLAGES AT 'GHOST'S HOLE'

The reservoir at Poulaphouca was created in the 1930s and early 1940s by the damming of the River Liffey as part of a joint project by the ESB and Dublin City Council to build a second hydro-electric power station in Ireland while at the same time the reservoir created as a result would be used to supply water to Dublin city and its surroundings.

Poulaphouca (from the Irish *Poll na Phúca* meaning 'The Ghost's Hole') takes its name from the small village of that name situated at the south-western corner of the reservoir where the dam is situated. At the time of its creation, the waters of the reservoir submerged a number of villages. (A 12th century Cross is today situated in the town cemetery, having been moved there when its original site was flooded). Today, the reservoir provides amenity facilities for pastimes such as fishing, rowing and sailing. The area has also been designated a Special Protection Area by the National Parks and Wildlife Service and is known internationally for its Greylag Goose population. Situated on the edge of the Wicklow Mountains it is bounded by a fine road which

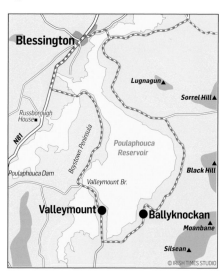

The Old Steam Tram terminus on the N81.

39

> *'From the bridge the road winds south and then southeast under the shadow of a succession of hills of ever increasing height.'*

The old Hydro electric dam at Poulaphouca.

travels around most of the edge of the reservoir and which is our route today.

We began our exploration from the busy town of Blessington which was at one time the terminus of the Dublin and Blessington Steam Tramway. Blessington's tree-lined main street was laid out in the 1680s by Michael Boyle, Archbishop of Dublin, and was once an important staging post for coaches traveling between Dublin and Carlow. In 1895 a four and a half mile extension of the tramway to the village of Poulaphouca was opened. Although the operation of the steam trams came to an end in 1932, the old ticket office still exists located on the eastern side of the N81 where it once overlooked the 150 ft high Poulaphouca Waterfall. Today, due to the construction of the dam, little water flows over this once renowned waterfall.

Turning westwards off the main street of Blessington at the signpost for Kilbride the road winds downhill under a canopy of trees to the Blessington Bridge which crosses to the eastern side of the reservoir. From the bridge the road winds south and then southeast under the shadow of a succession of hills of ever increasing height: Lugnagun (446 m.), Sorrel Hill (599 m.), Black Hill (602 m.) and Moanbane (703 m.). Along the way the road passes through the pleasant village of

The bridge over the Reservoir at Boystown Upper.

Lacken before swinging around a wide bay to the southwest and into the village of Ballyknocken.

A few kilometres southwest of Ballyknocken, turn north on the R758 which soon passes through Valleymount with its curious St. Joseph's Church, built in 1803 and with a facade designed by Mexican immigrants. Shortly after Valleymount a bridge takes us across to the Boystown Peninsula and it is here that the best views across the reservoir

The blue waters of Poulaphouca Reservoir.

are to be had looking east towards the Wicklow Mountains.

Before long the road turns west and once again we cross a bridge which leads to the junction with the N81. Before turning northeast and returning to Blessington, take the time to divert southwest along the N81 *via* Russborough House and as far as the Poulaphouca bridge and the hydro-electric dam.

This is an unusual drive with plenty of opportunity for short, interesting diversions to be enjoyed at a leisurely pace and hopefully on a fine day which shows off the surrounding countryside at its magnificent best.

10. *Muckish Mountain Drive*

MIGHTY MUCKISH!

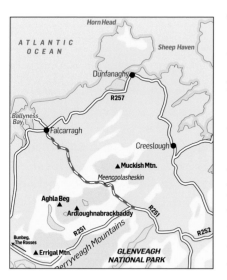

The north-west coast of Donegal is a coast of contrasts – the landscape revealing incredible variation as one journeys from Bunbeg to Creeslough via Gortahork, Falcarragh and Dunfanaghy. It also incorporates one of my favourite mountain roads – Muckish mountain pass that runs from Falcarragh and on towards Letterkenny – and having not driven this road in many years I was anxious to rediscover its charms.

Falcarragh, with its neo-gothic church dating back to 1792, was our starting point. This is the heart of the area known as 'The Rosses' where aspects of traditional Irish life which have long since disappeared elsewhere are preserved and where Irish is still spoken. The Muckish drive is signposted from the center of Falcarragh village, which lies on the edge of Ballyness Bay. Nearby in the grounds of Ballyconnell House is the Cloghaneely Stone, about which there are many legends. Tradition says it was on this stone that Baldor, the one-eyed King of nearby Tory Island, decapitated the local chieftain, MacKineely.

Muckish Mountain and the quarry operating on its slopes.

The village is dominated by Errigal (752m) to the south and Muckish (666m) to the south-east, and the road across the Muckish Gap rises slowly at first as it leaves Falcarragh. On the day of our passage across the Gap, cloud obscured the heights of Muckish Mountain. Away to the south of the road, Aghla Beg rises to 564m while nearby Ardloughnabrackbaddy is 603m high.

43

'The simple fact is that one of the most beautiful landscapes in north-west Donegal which we hold in trust for future generations has been disfigured in this way'

Shrouded in cloud — mighty Muckish.

Although the higher Muckish remained clouded, these two were revealed in all their mountain finery.

This is a place of very great natural beauty and it was a shock, therefore, to see a gate on a road leading off our road, to a land-fill site, admittedly now closed. It was hard to credit that a local authority could desecrate such an area of sublime beauty. But worse was to follow. As we reached the highest point of the Gap at Meencoolasheskin a huge lighter coloured gash in the side of Muckish Mountain revealed itself to apparently be a large quarry.

While I'm quite sure there is a local history concerning both these sites, the simple fact is that one of the most beautiful landscapes in north-west Donegal which we hold in trust for future generations has been disfigured in this way. The placing of a land-fill facility here is beyond comprehension while the allowing of large scale-quarrying at Muckish is almost equally hard to comprehend. In all my travels throughout the length and breath of this island, nowhere have I encountered such disregard for our heritage.

The road to Muckish.

Doing my best to ignore these issues for a moment, Muckish Gap once again wove its magic on me as we began the long slow descent towards the junction with the R251 on the edge of the beautiful Glenveagh National Park and the road to Letterkenny.

Yet, I left this road deeply saddened by what I had seen, and fearful for the future of the most beautiful locations on this island. Bad as it is that such as a land-fill site and a quarry should be allowed on Muckish Mountain but that they should also be sited on the edge of Glenveagh National Park –surely one of the most beautiful places on this island – is nothing short of a national disgrace.

However, look for yourself, travel the beautiful Muckish Gap and decide for yourself, but do it soon, before its made worse.

Wayside shrine at Meencoolasheskin.

11. Sorrel Hill

IN THE HEART OF WICKLOW

While in the area around Poulaphouca Reservoir one road on my map simply cried out to be explored. This is the road from Lacken which climbs into the heart of the Wicklow Mountains and curls around Sorrel Hill before winding its way back to the upper reaches of Poulaphouca Reservoir.

Lacken is a pretty village beautifully situated on the eastern shore of the reservoir. A fork in the road from Blessington Bridge to Valleymount as it runs through the village is the start of our route and climbs steeply up as it heads due east.

As it climbs the road reveals the u-shaped Kilbeg valley and Black Hill (602 m) to the south. There are numerous places to stop and admire

Looking south-west towards Vallymount from the base of Sorrel Hill.

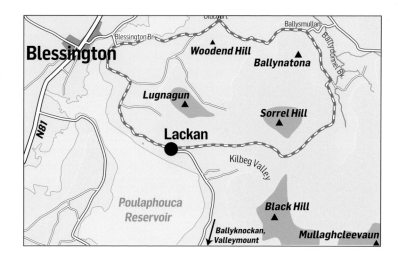

'Not for the first time, one marvels that such wildness should be so close to and so accessible to this island's most densly populated city.'

To the north as we round Sorrel Hill the RTE mast at Kippure acts as a landmark visble for many miles.

the fine vistas which open up over the reservoir towards Valleymount in particular but it is the views to the south east in particular, towards Mullaghcleevaun (849 m), East Top (795 m), Duff Hill (729 m), Gravale (718 m) and Carrigvore (682 m) that really excite the senses.

This is the heart of Wicklow and on the day of my exploration several of the hills still wore a mantle of winter snow. From our vantage point on the road around Sorrel Hill the nearest slopes are wooded and gradually give way to a more barren mountainscape in the distance. Not for the first time, one marvels that such wildness should be so close to and so accessible to this island's most densly populated city.

For such an exposed mountain road, its remarkable that our road is in such good condition. By the time it turns northwards and runs alongside the Ballydonnell Brook – a tributary of the River Liffey – it has begun to enter a more sheltered landscape. There's plenty to explore here if you so desire and the RTE mast on Kippure (757 m) acts as a reference point seemingly visible from everywhere along our route.

The northern end of the lake from Sorrel Hill.

Traveling north and then east the landscape changes quite quickly becoming less exposed and more gentle and we continue to bear left at the junctions at Ballysmullan and Oldcourt as we circumnavigate the base of Ballynatona (408 m) and Woodend Hill (302 m). From Oldcourt the road soon joins the edge of the northern end of the reservoir and before long we reach Blessington Bridge.

This whole area is particularly rich in prehistoric remains and if you've a mind to explore on foot, there are cairns atop Sorrel Hill, Lugnagun and Woodend Hill where there are two. Close to the start of our journey there's a megalithic tomb to the north on the slopes between Sorrel Hill and Lugnaguan.

This is a relatively short journey but in its short distance provides some truly spectacular views first over the Poulaphouca Reservoir and then into the very heartland of wildest Wicklow towards Duff Hill and Mullaghcleevaun. Don't attempt it in winter – choose one of the bright clear spring days we're experiencing at the moment and you'll be rewarded with some of the views that make Wicklow so special.

12. Loughcrew to Fore

BY THE HILL OF THE WITCH

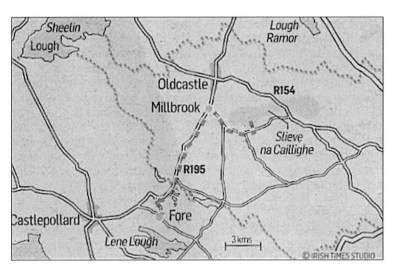

We all have our favorite roads. They are favorites because we like the scenery thay take us through or because we simply enjoy driving them. For me they are roads that excite the senses and that bring alive the best characteristics of whatever car I happen to be driving. In this series I've sometimes come across roads like that but which are either too short or have neither a sufficiently interesting history or landscape to make them worth including. The subject of this weeks article is relatively short but as it joins together two of my favorite places then it simply had to find its way into this series on 'Great Roads'.

The car park at Loughcrew Passage Tombs close to Oldcastle in County Meath is our starting point and is signposted from the Kells to Oldcastle road. I discovered *Slieve na Caillighe* – literally the Hill of the Witch – many years ago. It's a wonderful place, perched on the highest hilltops in County Meath, and part of the triangle of Neolithic remains found at Newgrange, Four Knocks and Loughcrew. There are

Hot-air balloons over Loughcrew,
starting point of this exploration.

St Féichín's Church on the slopes of the southern side of Fore Valley contains the only Anchorite cell in Ireland.

> '*While nothing special for the first few kilometres, this road soon acquires a character which sets it apart from most other roads in the area.*'

traces of no less than 25 tombs here and the most important, on Carnbane East, is a classic cross-shaped chamber into which, on the equinox days of March 21st and September 21st, the sun enters to illuminate the series of radial line patterns carved on many of the stones inside the tomb.

Heading south from the car park we quickly arrive on the main road and turn west past the derelict lodge of Loughcrew House towards Millbrook. From here, on summer evenings, one can often watch balloonists take to the skies over Loughcrew in their hot-air balloons. Joining the Oldcastle to Castlepollard road (R195) we again turn south towards the Valley of Fore.

While nothing special for the first few kilometres, this road soon acquires a character which sets it apart from most other roads in the area. Well-surfaced, it rises and falls and begins to flow in a manner guaranteed to excite the most traffic-weary driver. All too soon, however, we come to the signpost for Fore and we leave the R195 to take the short road into the tiny village of Fore.

The Valley of Fore is an extraordinary place. For Ireland, the landscape is unusual with its jagged rocky outcrops exposed on the hillsides of an otherwise verdant valley. Right in the centre of the valley lies the ruins of Fore Abbey which was founded in 630 AD and where more than 300 monks are said to have resided. There are also the ruins of a Benedictine Priory founded some-

Loughcrew Lodge, derelict on the slopes of the Loughcrew hills.

Fore Abbey, centrepiece of historic Fore Valley.

time before 1200 by the de Lacys and which represents the most extensive remains of any Benedictine house in Ireland.

Particularly fascinating amongst the many ruins in the valley of Fore is the Anchorite's Cell. This is located in the tower of St Féichín's Church on the slopes of the southern side of Fore Valley. The cell was used by a religious person who upon entering it made a vow never to leave it during the rest of his life and it is believed to be the only such cell in Ireland.

The tower containing the cell dates back to the 15th century although the site on which it is built is much older. In the 17th century the church was partially converted into a mausoleum by the local Greville-Nugent family.

What better way to spend half a day that by exploring these two wonderful places and enjoying the road which links them.

13. From Thomastown to St Mullins

A TALE OF TWO SISTERS

Regard this journey as a Sunday drive for it links together some of Ireland's prettiest villages as it zigzags around the dominant features of this landscape – the Rivers Nore and Barrow – two of the 'Three sisters'.

We began our journey at Thomastown turning off the busy N9, forsaking its 18th century bridge and instead taking the road for Inistioge along the banks of the River Nore. I wish I could say that there are spectacular views of the river as the road winds along beside it but as so often in Ireland the views are hidden by high hedges. (Some have unkindly suggested that the views would be visible if I were driving something other than a Lotus but I've checked and can confirm that it makes little difference!) Crossing the River Nore we enter into the village of Inistioge with its ten-arched bridge, ruined castle and 18th and 19th century houses and streetscape. It's a pretty place with a

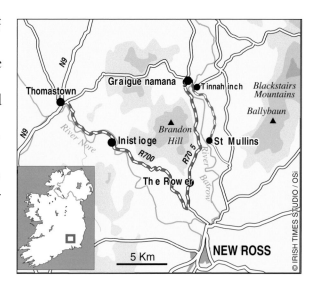

The valley of the River Barrow. To the left of the river can be seen the ruins and motte at St Mullins.

55

The pretty village of Inistioge has a cosmopolitan air unusual in Irish villages.

> *'One gets the overpowering sensation of steamy growth, of success over nature, of peace as unbroken as the buzzing of bees.'* SEAN O FAOLÁIN

surprisingly cosmopolitan aspect derived from its roadside bars and cafes grouped beside its grassy square. As a backdrop, Brandon Hill, topped by a cairn, rises in the background. An unusual feature are the Catholic and Protestant churches tucked away together and divided only by a graveyard.

Continue now along the R700 past Woodstock Gardens and Arboretum (which were created by Lady Louisa Tighe) for several kilometres until turning left at the sign for the village inn quaintly named The Rower. We now follow the R705 to Graiguenamanagh. All along this road are views across the valley of the River Barrow towards the Blackstairs Mountains rising in the distance, Mount Leinster and Blackstair Mountain being the most prominent peaks.

Before long the valley becomes heavily forested before dropping down to Graiguenamanagh (the 'dwelling of the monks'). Here the rivers Blackwater and Barrow meet and are crossed by George Semple's seven-arched 18th century bridge. Here also, reminding us once again of their hold on this area in times long gone, is a ruined Norman castle. Despite its modern bustle there is a peace and tranquility, a timelessness everywhere in this valley which was perhaps best spoken of

The ruins of some of the monastic churches at St Mullins crowd beside the old Church of Ireland.

by Séan O'Faoláin: *"The whole valley swoons in an air so delicately moist that it seems too heavy to move, so that on wet days even the clouds lie asleep across distant mountains, and one gets the overpowering sensation of steamy growth, of success over nature, of peace as unbroken as the buzzing of bees."*

Nowhere in this beautiful valley was this more apparent that in St Mullins, the end of our journey. As we left Graiguenamanagh over its high backed bridge and crossed into the village of Tinnahinch we turned right to follow the signs for St Mullins taking us once again along the road nearest the river.

St Mullins, or St Moling's House, is a place steeped in history which enchants with its tranquility and sense of being far removed from our world. St Moling here founded a monastic settlement and today the ruins of four or five churches are visible together with the base of a round tower and a small oratory. These ruins are grouped close to a church of much more recent origin, now apparently no longer in use and surrounded on the southwestern side by a graveyard which contains the last resting place of many who died in the Rising of 1798. Once again the Norman hand on the landscape is felt here as a motte rises in front of the graveyard. Finish your journey in St Mullins by exploring these ancient sites at this bend in the River Barrow, silent witness to our history.

14. Limavady to Downhill

THE BISHOP'S ROAD

On this journey we've headed almost to the northern tip of Ulster and traveled the road from just outside Limavady to the pretty seaside hamlet of Downhill, close to Castlerock on the northern coast.

Leaving Limavady on the B201 road to Coleraine we turned off at the signpost for Downhill about 4 kilometres from the town. Having turned off the B201 the road travels through a rural landscape for 2 to 3 kilometres before rising quickly onto the plateau which we plan to traverse. The road surface – as throughout this route – is very good and reminds one once again of the excellent pothole-free minor roads that criss-cross Ulster in sharp contrast to the poor condition of the majority of the Republic's equivalent roads.

As the road heads between Binevenagh and Ballyhanna Forests the view to the west across Lough Foyle to the Inishowen Peninsula is spectacular while

The painted houses at Downhill are an unexpected sight tucked away at the foot of the cliff at the end of the Bishop's Road.

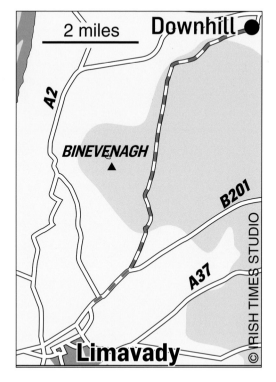

59

Our Daimler SP250 provided comfortable motoring in true 'Grand Touring' style.

Magilligan Strand stretches roughly from north to south for a considerable distance. Magilligan Strand is steeped in transport history and was the scene of some of the early flights of the first man to fly in Ireland, Harry Ferguson. In the early days of motoring it was also the scene of speed trials as part of the Irish Automobile Club Reliability Trials which were such important events in the proving of early cars.

About 4¹/₂ kilometres along the road there is a turn-off to the northwest and from it a forest road leads down to parking areas beside Binevenagh Lake from where there are once again spectacular views across Lough Foyle. Close by, Binevenagh Mountain rises to 373

'In the early days of motoring (Magilligan Strand) was also the scene of speed trials as part of the Irish Automobile Club Reliability Trials which were such important events in the proving of early cars.'

The spectacular Mussenden Temple in its cliff-top location.

metres. Binevenagh, incidentally, means 'terrifying promontory'.

Back on the road across the plateau we pass Windy Hill shortly after which the road changes direction and begins to head north east. From here the view across to Inishowen Head dominates before the road begins to descend to the tiny hamlet of Downhill with its painted row of houses on the coast. The last part of the road descends sharply to join the coastal A2 route.

Just up the road stands the ruins of Downhill Castle, built in the 18th century for Frederick Harvey, 4th Earl of Bristol, who became Bishop of Derry in 1768 and who, because of his two titles, was known as the Earl Bishop. And he it was who caused the road we have just traversed to be built as well. Today, the castle is in ruins, having been burnt down in 1851, but another of his creations, the splendid Mussenden Temple, survives in its cliff-top setting having been built in 1785 as a summer library by the Earl Bishop. It is in fact a copy of the Temple of Vesta at Tivoli, having been admired by the Earl Bishop during his many travels. Its pillared and domed rotunda bears an inscription written by Lucretius and translated by Dryden.

Tis pleasant safely to behold from shore,
The rolling ship and hear the tempest roar.

The Earl Bishop was also responsible for the nearby beautiful Downhill Forest where he caused many rare trees to be planted amongst its many waterfalls and prehistoric mound, Dungannon Hill.

This is an unexpectedly spectacular and interesting drive in a corner of Ulster that we have not explored in our previous drives. Don't miss it.

15. Killarney to Kenmare

CLASSIC KERRY

For many years, as Killarney played host annually to the Circuit of Ireland Rally, one road was synonymous with the event – Moll's Gap – the classic stage run over the Killarney to Kenmare road via the famous pass. Run early on the Sunday morning of the event, to be one of the thousands of spectators on Moll's Gap was an experience to be savoured as top rally drivers demonstrated their skills on this demanding test of driver and car.

Today, Moll's Gap is better known as the starting point of many tourist journeys around the famous Ring of Kerry. As a result many choose to avoid it for quieter, less traveled roads though the Kerry landscape. However, to do so is to miss out on one of the great roads in Kerry; a road which has much to offer the enthusiastic driver.

To enjoy Moll's Gap at its best, leave the bustling town of Killarney by the N71 early in the morning before the tourist coaches begin their never-ending circuits of the

As it climbs to Moll's Gap, the road passes through this rock arch. All along this section the rock face runs down to the edge of the road itself.

Evidently, Kerry has some road hazards unique to itself. You have been warned!

'But as you travel its course, spare a moment's thought for its ghosts. Pause and recall the sounds of fast cars driven by some of the great names of rallying.'

Ring of Kerry. Heading out past Muckcross House, one travels through the Killarney National Park; it's vast 27,000 acres enclosing three lakes and the surrounding mountains and woods. This is one of the last remnants of Ireland's primeval countryside and red deer roam freely through its oak and yew woodlands. Along this section, the road takes on the essential character which it retains to the top of Moll's Gap. Smooth, with an excellent surface, the road quickly develops a rhythm as it twists left and right, rising and falling on the gentle climb past the picturesque Lough Leane and smaller Muckcross Lake. To your right, Tomies Mountain (733m) and Purple Mountain (832m) rise against a backdrop of the impressive MacGillycuddy Reeks. On the other side rises Torc Mountain (535m) and behind it Mangerton Mountain some 300 metres higher. Along this section of the road the rock-face runs down to the edge of the tarmac, the site of many retirements in past Circuit of Ireland rallies by drivers who failed to give this stretch of road the respect it demands. Here too, the road passes through an arch cut through the rock when the original road was built.

The twistest part of the run to the pass follows and now, providing the early morning mist has cleared, one can look out over the Upper Lake and the famous Ladies View. Soon after, one passes over Moll's Gap itself and begins the descent into Kenmare.

Immediately, as so often is the case, the character of the road changes on this side of the mountains. Here, on the descent, the landscape is no longer clothed in trees as on the Killarney side of the pass, giving a much more windswept aspect to the road as it clings to the edge of the mountainside. Finally, Peekeen Mountain (554m) rises on your left as the descent into Kenmare continues.

As the N71 climbs out of Killarney through the Killarney National Park, the road takes on the essential character which it retains to the top of the pass.

In all the N71 from Killarney to Kenmare winds its way along 32 kms of twisting, winding road with an excellent surface and some of the most famous views in Ireland. But as you travel its course, spare a moment's thought for its ghosts. Pause and recall the sounds of fast cars driven by some of the great names of rallying over this most Irish of special stages – the classic Moll's Gap.

THE CIRCUIT OF IRELAND RALLY

Established as the Ulster Motor Rally as far back as 1931, the 1950s – 1970s were the great days of the annual Circuit of Ireland Rally. Classic special stages in the Wicklow Mountains and in Kerry and West Cork gave the event a character unlike any other international rally. In the 1990s various changes to the international rules changed the event so that it became a shadow of the challenge it had once been. However, memories of the 'greats' who contested the event remain with all those fortunate enough to have seen them in action.

Irish Rally legend Billy Coleman in action in a Lancia Stratos on the Circuit of Ireland. Photo courtesy Ian Lynas.

16. Louisburg to Leenaun R335

THE PERFECT DRIVE

It would be hard to imagine a more perfect drive through a spectacular Irish landscape than the road which takes you from Louisburg, beside Clew Bay, to Leenaun, at the head of spectacular Killary Harbour. This road has everything. Spectacular mountains and lakes, a landscape little touched by human hands (the R335 itself is almost the only sign of human intervention) and a series of ever-more spectacular vistas, while the road itself offers a driving experience which will live long in the memory.

Louisburg's Irish name is *Cluain Cearbán* meaning 'meadow of buttercups' but it was renamed by the Marquess of Sligo to honour an uncle who had played a significant part in the capture in 1758 of the French fortress of Louisbourg on Cape Breton Island in Nova Scotia. It's a pretty town, much of it having been laid out in the 18th century and a good starting place for our journey.

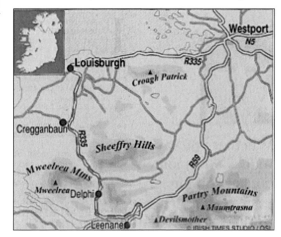

From Louisburg, turn onto the R335 signposted for Leenaun and Delphi. Ireland's holy mountain, Croagh Patrick, rises some 762 metres on your left while ahead the landscape is flush with yellow gorse and in

The R335 hugs the eastern shore of Lough Doo as it heads towards Leenaun.

The poignant Famine Cross which recalls the hungry poor who walked this landscape in the late 1840's.

the distance rise the Sheeffry Hills (climbing to an identical 762 metres) and the Mweel Rea Mountains which have as their highest point, Mweelrea, at 814 metres.

After some 10 kilometres Doo Lough and the smaller Glencullen Lough are reached and the road drops down beside the eastern shore of the lake. Here is a poignant Famine cross remembering the hungry poor who walked this landscape in the late 1840s as well as those hungry poor who still walk this world today.

This is a spot of spectacular beauty framed by the craggy slopes of Ben Bury to the west of the lough and Barrclashcame which slopes down to the edge of the R335. Near the southern end of the lough is the turn signposted for Cummin which takes you onto the road featured some time ago in the second of this series.

Our path, however, lies south and we head into the Delphi Valley. Delphi is a magical place, so named by the 2nd Marquess of Sligo – who was Byron's traveling companion in Greece – and who built a fishing lodge here in the 1830s naming it Delphi as it so reminded him of the site of the Oracle at Delphi in Greece. Close by Delphi is the small Fin Lough which we pass before the road takes us south to the northern side of Killary Harbour.

Killary Harbour, of course, is not a harbour at all but rather a long, narrow inlet that forms Ireland's only real fiord as it winds in from the Atlantic forming a natural border between Mayo and Galway on its way to meet the outflow of the River Erriff. Its safe deep-water anchorage pro-

A great car, a great road and great driving memories which will live long in the mind's eye.

'This is a truly spectacular drive that will linger long in the memory calling you back.'

and Galway on its way to meet the outflow of the River Erriff. Its safe deep-water anchorage provides a dark brooding presence as the R335 now follows along its shore towards the village of Leenaun just south of the inlets tip on the Galway side.

This is a truly spectacular drive that will linger long in the memory calling you back. Allow plenty of time when you travel it to soak up its grandeur and isolation made accessible by the R335.

17. Glenariff Drive

THE QUEEN OF THE ANTRIM GLENS

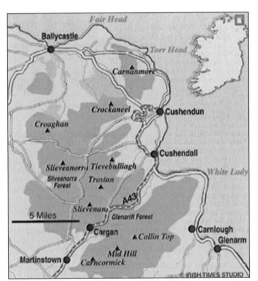

Glenariff opens out towards Red Bay with the village of Waterfoot visible in the distance.

There are nine Glens of Antrim of which Glenariff, where we begin our journey, has bestowed on it the additional title 'Queen of the Glens'. Described by the Writer William Thackeray as 'Switzerland in miniature', Glenariff is a spectacular glen, a classic U-shaped valley created by a glacier and with many tumbling waterfalls dropping down to feed the river of the same name that flows along its valley bottom.

By way of contrast to our usual transport we traveled by means of a true Grand Tourer, Audi's 4.2 litre A8 quattro, and incidentally, a turbo diesel, an indication of just how far diesel engines have progressed in recent years. Begin this journey by taking the A43 out of Ballymena and head for McGregor's Corner (marked by a Peugeot dealership) and on through the hamlet of Martinstown. To the east of the road rise the gentle slopes of Carncormick (436m) while to the north rise Slievenanee (540m) and Trostan (551m). Having passed through the village of Cargan, the landscape takes on a bleaker, more mountainous grassy aspect, with streams cutting deep into it's earth. Meeting a junction with the B14, stay with the A43, ignoring the signs for the 'Scenic Drive'. Hidden in the trees just to the left at this junction is the ruined Parkmore railway station, which was opened in 1876 and was one of the highest railway stations in Britain or Ireland. Originally, the narrow gauge Ballymena, Cushendall & Red Bay Railway

In many places the road winds along the Glen's spectacular slopes.

'Described by the Writer William Thackeray as 'Switzerland in miniature', Glenariff is a spectacular glen, a classic U-shaped valley created by a glacier.'

transported iron ore through here before becoming a tourist route after the ore was exhausted in 1889.

The glen now shows its most attractive face and a short excursion can be made to Glenariff Forest Park from where some of the best views of the area can be seen. Back on the A43 again, one begins to descend and a spectacular view to the sea opens up with the village of Waterfoot at the head of Red Bay. Soon, the A43 meets the A2 along the coast and turns for the pretty village of Cushendall passing through 'The Red Arch' along the way. In the main street of the village watch for the left turn as the A2 continues through Glencorp – the Glen of the Slaughtered, so named for reasons I was unable to discover – towards Cushendun via the Glendun Viaduct.

Turning west from Glencorp the road crosses the Dun river on a magnificent high viaduct known locally simply as 'The Big Bridge'. Designed by Charles Lanyon, the architect of Queen's University, Belfast, the bridge was built between 1834 and 1839 with all the stone for its construction being drawn from the Layde quarry near Cushendaun by horse and cart. It really is a most impressive structure and a short diversion will take one to its base from where it can be better appreciated.

'Johann' – A sculpture commemorating the last victim of the 2001 outbreak of Foot and Mouth disease.

Having crossed the viaduct the road twists and turns its way gently climbing before dropping once more as it comes closer to the attractive village of Cushendun. Owned by the National Trust and with an unusual Cornish-style architecture, Cushendun was the work of Clough Williams Ellis – who also designed the village of Portmeirion in Wales - between 1912 and 1925 for Lord Cushendun.

We ended our journey at the waters edge in Cushendun beside an unusual and poignant memorial, a sculpture of the goat 'Johann', commemorating the last animal to be culled in the Foot and Mouth outbreak of Spring 2001.

The Glens of Antrim, of which we have journeyed over but a few, are superb motoring roads well worth exploring and discovering for oneself. Journey over them and you will not be disappointed.

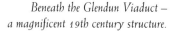

Beneath the Glendun Viaduct – a magnificent 19th century structure.

18. Newtownards to Strangford

ALONG STRANGFORD'S VARIED BANKS

Ireland's landscape, I am constantly reminded, is incredibly varied. There are the roads through areas of well-known natural beauty. Then there are the roads that have to be sought out and finally there are the roads we travel daily and from which it is necessary to take a step back to truly appreciate their natural beauty. Now, I'm not for one moment suggesting that those drivers for whom their daily commute takes them along the eastern shore of Strangford Lough don't appreciate its wonderful character – just that one needs to step back to gain a true appreciation of what a wonderful drive this is.

Even on the dull and overcast day we choose – for once a rare occasion on this Irish Summer – to drive from Newtownards to Portaferry, this is a route to surprise and delight. The whole Ards Peninsula separates Strangford Lough from the sea and in doing so creates a wonderfully varied place. The lough itself is a designated area of special scientific interest and its mudflats and salt marshes provide a safe haven for the many migratory birds that are to be found here.

A view from the western side of Strangford Lough across several of its many small islands.
Photo courtesy of
County Down Tourism.

'Dilly, dally along this road and enjoy its natural and man-made variety.'

The pretty town of Strangford across the lough from Portaferry has a 16th century tower house nestled behind its painted shorefront houses.

There is a regular ferry service from Strangford to Portaferry.

There are also a number of places along this route of special interest, the first of which is Mount Stewart. This is the 98-acre estate of the Londonderry family and the 18th century house contains a magnificent collection of works of art. Impressive as these are it is the World Heritage Garden, that was planted as a 'green fairyland' by Edith, Lady Londonderry, in the 1920s, and which ranks as one of Ireland's great gardens, which will impress. I have to admit that as one with little or no interest in ornate gardens I found this garden deeply impressive.

A little further along the A20 is the village of Grey Abbey, which takes its name from the 12th century Cistercian monastery now in ruins and regarded as one of the finest examples of Anglo-Norman ecclesiastical architecture on the island of Ireland. The ruins are fully accessible by the public and well worth the short detour. The village of Grey Abbey itself is notable for its many antique shops.

Continuing along the A20 towards Portaferry there are many views over the lough to the multitude of small islands on the western side, before the road passes through the village of Kircubbin and a short while later goes inland, although almost never out of sight of the lough, for a couple of kilometers before entering Portaferry.

Portaferry contains a castle built on a rocky outcrop by Sir Roland Savage around 1500 to guard the entrance to Strangford Lough. Today, it's a pleasant small town that's served by a regular car ferry from the town of Strangford, visible about two kilometers across the mouth of Strangford Lough. The ferry serves as a journey-saving route to Downpatrick and on to Newry. The neck of

The castle of the Savages nestles amongst the streets and painted houses of Portaferry.

the lough, between Portaferry and Strangford, is shaped like a venturi and as a consequence speeds up the flow of water into and out of Strangford Lough. At times when the tide is turning this can produce strong eddies and even whirlpools easily visible from the ferry.

Dilly, dally along this road and enjoy its natural and man-made variety. Allow yourself plenty of time, as there's much to see that's worthwhile.

There are reputed to be as many as 365 islands and peninsulas on Strangford Lough.

19. Slieve Gullion

REDISCOVERING SOUTH ARMAGH

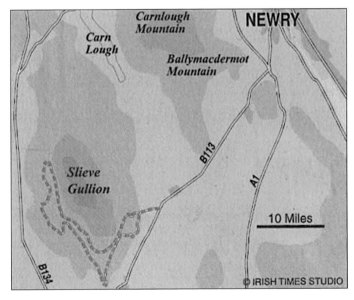

Slieve Gullion's slopes provide wonderful views across South Armagh's surprising landscape.

The 'Troubles' were not kind to South Armagh, but the years since the Good Friday Agreement have worked wonders for this neglected area where there is much for the motorist to discover. Perhaps the most dramatic and scenic part of South Armagh is the area around Slieve Gullion (Holly Mountain) just a few short kilometres south-west of Newry. Surprisingly few people are familiar with this ancient mountain which is mentioned in the epic *The Cattle Raid of Cooley*. At its 576 metre summit – the highest in Armagh - is a 5,000 year-old passage grave and nearby is the small *Calliagh Bernas Lough* – The Witch's Lake – which is associated with the enchantment of Finn McCool by a witch.

Approaching from Dublin along the newly extended M1 continue to the junction for Newry. Turning right will bring you into the town of Newry but turning left will take you along the B113 through the village of Meigh and shortly afterwards to the modest entrance to Slieve Gullion Forest Park. A short drive takes you to the Courtyard Buildings which were originally built by the Chambre family in 1820 and are now managed by The Slieve Gullion Courtyard Development Group, who provide environmental education and tourist facilities.

'The mountains of the Cooley Peninsula and the Mournes rise up in the distance to provide a spectacular backdrop to the rolling countryside of south Armagh.'

The entrance to Slieve Gullion Forest park is by way of a narrow, leafy lane.

Signposted from the Courtyard car park is the thirteen kilometre Slieve Gullion Drive which is one-way throughout its length. For the first kilometre or two the road takes you through a heavily wooded area before breaking out into open moorland which reveals the most spectacular views as the road rapidly ascends. The mountains of the Cooley Peninsula and the Mournes rise up in the distance to provide a spectacular backdrop to the rolling countryside of south Armagh.

As the road swings first north-west and then due north it reveals more spectacular views towards the rugged nearby hills of Slievenabolea, Carrickastickan and Croslieve

SLIEVE GULLION FOREST PARK

The Forest park is situated in an area of outstanding beauty on the slopes of Slieve Gullion Mountain that forms the focal point of the Ring of Gullion. The unspoilt rugged scenery owes its origin to a volcanic past some 60 million years ago followed by millions of years of weathering by ice and rain.

Today, the Park covers an area of 960 hectares of woodland and heather moorland. The Forest Service began planting in 1951 and the main trees are pine, spruce, larch and Douglas fir. The lower slopes of Slieve Gullion are mostly clothed in coniferous woodland, with small areas of old broadleaved woodland confined to the more sheltered and fertile areas. Between the upper edge of the Forest and the summit of Slieve Gullion, heather moorland predominates and Skylarks and Meadow pipits can be heard on this open area. There is a small herd of feral goats, and Irish hares can be seen occasionally.

The scenic thirteen kilometre long drive leads through the wooded lower slopes and emerges onto the upper moorland giving way to wonderful views of the surrounding countryside.

The Courtyard Buildings, originally built by the Chamber family in 1820, are now managed by the Slieve Gullion Courtyard Development Group, who provide environmental education and tourist facilities.

The nearby Walled Garden is laid out in an informal manner and comprises a variety of trees, shrubs and herbaceous plants, set around an ornamental pond.

– all reflecting, like Slieve Gullion itself - their origins in volcanic activity many millennia ago. While looking towards these spectacular hills a brief glimpse is caught of a Peregrine Falcon – the perfect addition to a magnificent landscape.

The Slieve Gullion Drive continues to its most northerly and highest point from where one can continue on foot to the passage grave on its summit. The road now doubles back on itself while descending all the while providing new and equally spectacular views and confirming the realisation that this is a very beautiful part of Ireland and one which the 'Troubles' kept from us for far too long.

Having reached its most southerly point the drive now swings back towards the north-east returning to the point where we began close to the Courtyard. All in all a drive of wonderful rediscovery and somewhere that will doubtless call us back again in the future.

20. *The Ballaghnabeama Gap*

A SECRET PLACE WORTH SEEKING OUT

The Ballaghbeama Gap has intrigued me since I came across a photograph taken around 1898 of a hardy – and adventurous – group of cyclists making their way through the rocky defile which forms the pass. It's a rugged, wild place in this old photograph and very different to any other road I had traveled in Ireland. It took me a while to find it's location for the original photograph gave no information other than it's name. Eventually, a search of the most likely locations revealed that it was situated on the Kenmare Peninsula close to the heart of the mighty Macgillycuddy Reeks and within sight of Ireland's highest mountain, the 1038m Carauntoohil.

A close study of the latest edition of the excellent Ordnance Survey of Ireland Discovery Series map of the area revealed that there appeared to be a car-navigitable road crossing the Gap. I decided to approach the Ballaghbeama Gap from the west as the whole interior of the Kenmare Peninsula looked inter-

Pausing in the stillness and rugged beauty of Ballaghnabeam Pass.

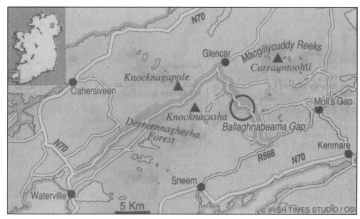

83

Crossing the gap at Ballaghisheen, the landscape unexpectedly stretches ahead in a lush but empty plain to the Macgillycuddy Reeks.

'In all I spent about half an hour there savouring its still, empty silence and wondering at the total lack of tourists here between the rocky heights of Mullaghanattin and Knockaunattin.'

esting on the map, seemingly sparsely populated and dotted with mountains which promised to make for an interesting road to travel. So it was that I turned off the N70 about 3 kilometers north of Waterville forsaking the tourist trail of the Ring of Kerry for I knew not what. I turned off the N70 at a crossroads marked by a church and followed the signposts for Glencar.

Initially, the road is fairly straight and is reasonably wide having the good surface which characterised the entire route I took. Soon, the scattered houses grew fewer and I began to realise that I had entered a part of The Kingdom very different from the better-known tourist locations. Over the next 20 kilometers I meet a postman's van and a single car. By then I had gently climbed through Derreennageeha Forest to Ballaghisheen, between the twin pillars of Knocknagapple (466m) and the higher Knocknausha. Crossing the gap at Ballaghisheen, the landscape unexpectedly stretched ahead of me in a lush but empty plain to the Macgillycuddy Reeks, reminiscent of some of the landscapes from Peter Jackson's

Intrepid party of cyclists at Ballaghnabeama circa. 1898.

As we travel towards the mighty Macgillycuddyreeks, Ireland's highest mountain, Carauntoohil, is visible ahead.

beloved New Zealand in 'The Lord of the Rings' film trilogy. The lack of any sign of habitation or other cars added to the pleasant illusion.

Turning south at a Y-junction signposted for Sneem and Killarney, I now began to travel through an area of considerably more roads, but clearly sign posted towards my destination. Climbing away from the Glashwee river the Ballaghbeama Gap came into sight, confirming it's identity by its very wildness, so evident in that century-old photograph. The Gap itself was soon reached and proved every bit as wild and rugged as hoped. In all I spent about half an hour there savouring its still, empty silence and wondering at the total lack of tourists here between the rocky heights of Mullaghanattin and Knockaunattin. Perhaps, the narrowness of the road – only sufficient for a single car although there are plenty of places to pull in to allow two cars pass – puts them off. If so, they are missing out on one of the most wonderful places I have discovered anywhere in Ireland.

After Ballaghbeama, I have to admit, the rest of the journey could only be an anti-climax as one descends down to the junction with the R568 leading to Moll's Gap or southwest to Sneem.

Seek out this road. It will reward your effort. But don't tell too many people. It's a Kerry secret!

21. Malin Head Drive

A SPECIAL PLACE

In the last article in the 2007 series we headed north to Donegal's Inishowen peninsula, and on to Ireland's most northerly tip, Malin Head, on a road of many contrasts.

Start on this tour of Malin Head from the pretty town of Malin on Trawbreaga Bay taking the R242 signposted for Lag and Malin Head. At first it's a pleasant road skirted by the seashore on your left but after a couple of kilometres it turns inland and the terrain quickly changes. To the east of the road Cranny Hill rises to 138m. while a short road to the left passes Lag Church in its unusual and solitary location and continues to Five-Fingers Beach, itself worthy of a short diversion.

Returning to the R242, a road marked with a brown 'Inishowen 100' sign leads sharply up

© IRISH TIMES STUDIO / OSI

The unusual location of the church at Lag with the R242 in the background.

87

Well worth the short diversion from the R242 – the beach at Five-Fingers.

'This is Donegal at its magnificent best and reminds one of just why this most northern of the Republic's counties is a special place to visit.'

Knockglass Hill, Soldiers Hill and on around a narrow but totally adequate coastal drive. The views on this section of the drive are magnificent looking across the entrance to Trawbreaga Bay towards Doagh Island (not actually an island) where a very large concentration of Megalithic remains are located in its eastern half. This is Donegal at its magnificent best and reminds one of just why this most northern of the Republic's counties is a special place to visit.

All too soon, the road drops down again to nearer sea level and rejoins the R242 just before another turn close to the Coastal Radio Station with its high mast. Take this road and follow it to the small car park at the most westerly point of the road on Malin Head itself. The views from here to the west are again impres-

A classic open sports car and the magnificence of Donegal – what more could a motorist wish for?

Magnificent view across Trawbreage Bay towards Doagh Island – not actually an island at all.

sive. Continue on to the most northerly point of the road, marked by a short road to a car park beside what appears to have once been a tower house style dwelling. Here are architectural relics of 'The Emergency' when the Battle for the North Atlantic was fought from the Northern Ireland side of nearby Lough Foyle. Also here is the word 'EIRE' spelt out in what were once white-washed stones as a sign to airmen that they were approaching the coastline of neutral Ireland. Today, the word 'Eire' is almost lost in a sea of lesser messages left over the intervening years by visitors to this spot.

Rejoining the road we return to the R242 at the tiny village of Bulbinbeg and begin to head back towards the town of Malin once more. Before coming to the point where we left the R242 near Lag Church the road travels once again through a surprisingly wide variation of landscape – a feature encountered again and again on our travels throughout Ireland. After Lag the road once more runs alongside the sea shore and as we head in the opposite direction we can appreciate new aspects of this spectacular bay.

22. Black Head

SIMPLY ANOTHER WORLD

It's been far too long since we last visited the Burren region on behalf of this column. One of the very first articles in the first series described the road at Ballyalban, which climbs through some of the most spectacular landscape at the heart of the Burren and which is still used annually (along with nearby Corkscrew Hill) as the venue for a very challenging motor sport hillclimb.

The Burren, from the Gaelic word *Boireann* meaning 'The Stoney District,' is an area of limestone rock covering some 50 square miles in north County Clare. It's a strange area, with a landscape quite unlike any other in Ireland, and consists of succession upon succession of limestone terraces, hidden amongst which are some rare flora, including several Alpine-Arctic types. The entire area is very rich in historical and archaeological sites including more than 90 megalithic tombs and portal dolmens as well as a number of very interesting ring forts – chief amongst them being the triple ring fort Cahercommaun on the edge of an inland cliff, and the exceptionally well-preserved Caherconnell Stone Fort.

All along the coastal Black Head road the limestone mountains sweep down in spectacular fashion to the sea.

There are many caves in the soft limestone rock, the most spectacular with access for the public being Ailwee

Cave, near Ballyvaughan, which was discovered as recently as 1940, and is well worth a visit as is The Burren Center at Kilfenora where one can gain a better understanding of this unique region.

We set out to continue our exploration of The Burren by way of the coast road which winds it way around Black Head and along the edge of the Burren to the west of the village of Ballyvaughan. Ballyvaughan, from the Gaelic *Baile Ui Bhuirne* – O'Beacháin's Town, is a pretty village which makes an ideal centre for exploring The Burren. Leaving the village we kept along the edge of Ballyvaughan Bay. Along this section of the road the lush vegetation obscures a lot of the views to sea but the limestone peaks of Cappanawalla (312m), Gleninagh (317m) and Murrooghtoohy North (314m) rise successively to the southwest of the road. As we near Black Head itself – marked by a lighthouse, the road clings to the edge of the mountains close to the shoreline.

'For those who want to extend their exploration further there's a left turn at Fanore which climbs up through a spectacular gorge.'

Thankfully, the entire Burren Region is a protected habitat.

Rounding Black Head the Aran Islands are clearly visible away to the west as the coast road turns to head south west. A short distance further on the road moves slightly inland, still bordered to the left by the limestone mountains which sweep down to meet it in spectacular fashion before reaching the small village of Fanore with it's attractive nearby beach. For those who want to extend their exploration further there's a left turn at Fanore which climbs up through a spectacular gorge, flowing alongside the path of the River Caher for a while before eventually meeting the N67.

Meanwhile, the coast road continues along the edge of the limestone mountains – now dominated by Slieve Elva (344m), and traveling through the village of Craggagh, before eventually turning away from the sea to head south east towards the town of Lisdoonvarna.

I can't recommend The Burren region enough for its different, other-worldly feel, and its many roads waiting to take you to new wonders of this utterly unique landscape. I hope to return again soon for a longer exploration.

The Cars

Early in the first series of 'Great Drives' it became apparent that there was great interest from readers in the cars I was using for the series. Initially, all of the first series was completed in my own Lotus Elise 111R, this being the first new Elise to be sold in the Republic of Ireland. At various times cars loaned by distributors were used such as the Audi A8 Quattro and the silver Lotus Exige 220 S, while my own 1963 Daimler SP250 was used whenever possible and when there was the likelihood of good weather. Finally, over the last three years, my replacement for the Lotus Elise, a red Lotus Exige 220 S, was used most often.

Lotus Elise 111R
The car that revived Lotus fortunes in the mid-1990s, this example is the 1.8 litre Toyota engined version, with revised body shape. As well as using it on the 'Great Drives' series I've toured Scotland's Wester Ross region in it and used it for an unforgettable exploration of the *Alpine Strasse*, the road that travels along the southern part of the Bavaian Alps and into Austria. Like any Lotus it provides superb feedback and gives an unforgettable driving experience.

Audi A8 Quattro
Audi's flagship at the time we used it to explore the Antrim Glens, it would have been hard to find a greater contrast to our more usual Lotus Elise. Powerful and comfortable it provided a magic-carpet ride to Glenarm, the 'Queen of the Glens' and back. But, superb as it undoubtedly was, its very insulation from the road was a disappointment. Maybe, I've been driving small sports cars for too long!

Daimler SP250 (Dart)
My favourite drive. I acquired my Daimler Dart some five years ago and have loved every moment of driving it. It's a real challenge and rewards forward thinking on the road. Still fast, comfortable and with lots of nice touches, it's a wonderful vehicle for touring with plenty of room for luggage and a warm, comfortable cockpit. Yet most of all, it's the wonderful sound of that Edward Turner designed V-8 engine which is a constant joyful soundtrack to your motoring which makes the Dart so memorable to drive.

BMW Z1
Conceived by BMW as a concept car to show off their technical prowess at the 1988 Frankfurt show, such was the interest by prospective buyers that BMW decided to put it into production with virtually no changes to the original concept. This included unique 'drop-down' doors and most of the running gear, including it's smooth 2.5 litre engine, from the BMW 325 together with a plastic body and some pretty advanced aerodynamics for the time. It was also notable for introducing the 'Z-link' rear suspension which transformed the handling of BMW cars. In all, just 8,000 LHD examples were built, the majority being sold in Germany and France while just 70 went to Britain and one to Ireland. Today, it's an unusual tourer, fast and comfortable with a whole host of unusual features not found on any other car, ensuring it of 'classic' status.

Lotus Exige 220 S
The Lotus Exige 220 S is akin to a hardcore version of the Elise 111R. Fully adjustable suspension, a limited slip differential and road holding to match anything else on the road make the Exige an unforgettable driving experience. One snag, however, is that the handling and roadholding are delivered in a manner that spoils you for driving any other car – they just can't match the Lotus. It may be an acquired taste and entry and exit may require a supple body and a certain knack but once experienced it will never be forgotten.

If you've enjoyed this book, you may also enjoy these Dreoilín titles…

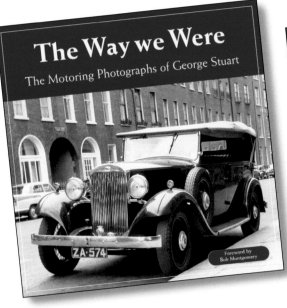

The Way we Were
The Motoring Photographs of George Stuart

Foreword by Bob Montgomery

ZA·574

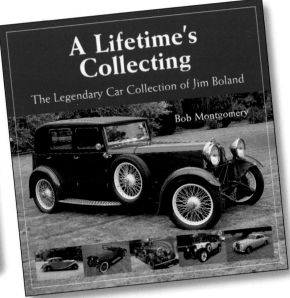

A Lifetime's Collecting
The Legendary Car Collection of Jim Boland

Bob Montgomery

Also Available:

The Dreoilín Transport Album Series

A range of inexpensive 32 page Albums featuring Irish Transport History and Personalities.

Titles include:

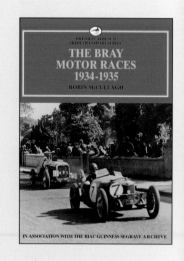

DREOILIN ALBUMS
IRISH TRANSPORT SERIES
THE BRAY MOTOR RACES 1934-1935
ROBIN McCULLAGH

IN ASSOCIATION WITH THE RIAC GUINNESS SEGRAVE ARCHIVE

See our full range of books at:
www.dreoilin.ie

Credit Card order-line at (00 353) 1 8354481